Flags of the Napoleonic Wars (1)

Colours, Standards and Guidons of France and her Allies

Terence Wise · Illustrated by Guido Rosignoli

Series editor Martin Windrow

First published in Great Britain in 1978 by Osprey Publishing,
Midland House, West Way, Botley, Oxford OX2 0PH, UK
44-02 23rd St, Suite 219, Long Island City, NY 11101, USA
Email: info@ospreypublishing.com

Transferred to digital print on demand 2010

First published 1978
8th impression 2005

Printed and bound by PrintOnDemand-Worldwide.com, Peterborough, UK

A CIP catalogue record for this book is available from the British Library

ISBN: 978 0 85045 171 9

Series Editor: Martin Windrow
Filmset by BAS Printers Limited, Over Wallop, Hampshire

FOR A CATALOGUE OF ALL BOOKS PUBLISHED BY
OSPREY MILITARY AND AVIATION PLEASE CONTACT:

Osprey Direct, c/o Random House Distribution Center,
400 Hahn Road, Westminster, MD 21157
Email: uscustomerservice@ospreypublishing.com

Osprey Direct, The Book Service Ltd, Distribution Centre,
Colchester Road, Frating Green, Colchester, Essex, CO7 7DW
Email: customerservice@ospreypublishing.com

www.ospreypublishing.com

Introduction

Throughout this book the various parts of the flags are referred to by their correct terms; i.e. the part nearest the pole is known as the hoist, the opposite edge being the fly. A canton is a square or corner of a flag, and always that corner next to the top of the pole. When the pole appears on the left edge of a flag, you are viewing the front or obverse of that flag; when it appears on the right edge you are seeing the rear or reverse of the flag. The pole is known as the stave, the metal 'spearhead' as the finial, and the metal shoe at the bottom end as the ferrule. The cords ending in tassels and tied beneath the finial are simply called cords, and the wide ribbons similarly placed are known as cravats. The main part of a flag is its field, and the various designs or devices are placed upon that field. The placing of devices on the field is sometimes described heraldically: the top left and bottom right are referred to as 1 and 4, the top right and bottom left as 2 and 3.

SOURCES

Ales, S. *L'Esercito del Regno Italico*

Andolenko, C. R. *Aigles de Napoléon contre Drapeaux du Tsar*

Bahrynowski, J. *Polish Infantry Uniforms of the Napoleonic Wars* (Article, Modelworld, February 1974)

Blankenhorn, E. *Guide to the Army Museum of Schloss Rastatt, Vol. 3*

Brunon, J. & R. *French Imperial & Italian Royal Eagles 1804–15* (Article, Alti Congresso 1º Internazionale)

Chelminski, J. *L'Armee du Duché de Varsovie, 1807–15*

Crociani, P. *Napoleon's Italian Army* (Series of articles in Tradition magazine)

Die Welt in Bildern. *Historische Fahnen (Album 8)*

Fallou, L. *La Garde Imperiale 1804–15*

Galliani, Parisini & Rocchiero. *La Cavalleria di linea Italica 1796–1814*

Ghisi, E. *Tricolore Italiano*

Hollander, O. *Nos Drapeaux et Etendards*

Lemonofides, D. *Standards from the Battlefield: Borodino* (Article, Battle magazine, December 1975)

Morris, R. O. *Colours and Standards of the Grand Duchy of Baden* (Article, Tradition, No 72)

Morris, R. O. *Colours of the Army of the Grand Duchy of Wurzburg* (Article, Tradition, No 57)

Over, K. *Flags and Standards of the Napoleonic Wars*

Pivka, Otto von. *Napoleon's German Allies: 1* (Men-at-Arms series)

Pivka, Otto von. *Napoleon's German Allies: 2* (Men-at-Arms series)

Plumet. *Plate Nos 52, 36, 34*

Rawkins, W. J. *Infantry Standards, Kingdom of Wurttemburg, 1811–14*

Rawkins, W. J. *Infantry & Cavalry Standards, Kingdom of Saxony, 1810–13*

Regnault, J. *Les Aigles Imperiales, 1804–15*

Rigondaud, A. *Lancers of the Vistula in Spain* (Article, Tradition, No 55)

Schild-Verlag. *German flags through history* (series of postcards)

The author also wishes to acknowledge the extensive research carried out on his behalf by Furio Lorenzetti of Milan on Italian and Neapolitan flags; and the assistance given by Otto von Pivka on flags of Bavaria and Saxony.

France

During the 1804–15 period the regiments of the French Army received flags of three patterns, each of which varied primarily in the individual inscriptions for each regiment and the shape or size according to the branch of the army, i.e. infantry, dragoons or cavalry. The first of these patterns was issued in 1804 but this issue took place simultaneously with that of the famous Napoleonic eagles, which relegated the flags to a comparatively

1 and 2. France: Front and rear of the 1804 model eagle of the 10th Regiment of Line Infantry.

minor role. We will therefore deal first with the eagles.

The eagle was chosen as the symbol of the French Army in the summer of 1804 by Napoleon himself, in preference to the ancient Gallic symbol of a cockerel. The Emperor's sculptor, Chaudet, made the original model, based on the Roman eagles, and from this were cast bronze copies in the workshop of Thomire. Each eagle was made of six parts: the body and head of two parts, joining face to back and including the left claw; the right claw; Jupiter's spindle; the hollow-section plinth, which was secured to the eagle by three screws; and the bottom of the plinth, with a 6cm socket into which fitted the stave, which was secured to the rest of the plinth by four screws. Each part was engraved with identification marks and individually finished with fine chisel work. Finally the numbers of the regiments were added to the front and back of the plinth.

The plinth was about 4cm high by 12cm long and the eagle and plinth together had an overall height of 308–310mm and a maximum width of 255mm. Weight was 1850 grams, or nearly four pounds. The eagle was carried on a blue stave approximately two metres in length.

The first of 560 eagles made in 1804 were presented on 5th December at the Champ de Mars in Paris by the Emperor, each regiment which received eagles making a solemn oath to defend them. The Guard was entitled to nineteen eagles and received thirteen at this presentation. (It is doubtful if the 2nd Regiments of Grenadiers and Chasseurs, raised in 1806, received eagles, while the Young Guard battalions were not entitled to them.) Line and Légère infantry regiments received one eagle per battalion, cavalry regiments one per squadron.

Other eagles were presented to regiments from time to time by the Emperor in the yard of the Tuileries, and it was very seldom that a general or even corps commander was allowed to make a presentation. Some regiments, particularly those formed in 1813 (all of which did not receive eagles) did, however, receive their eagles from the Ministry of War.

During the 1805 campaign some of the Hussar regiments, whose dispersed role was not conducive to confidence that they could honour their oath to defend the eagles, returned most of their eagles to their depots; and in September 1806 it was officially laid down that Hussar, Chasseurs à Cheval and Light Infantry regiments should hand in all their eagles at the beginning of a campaign. It is known that at least the 4th and 9th Hussars ignored this order and carried four eagles until 1812, and a Légère regiment's eagle was lost in battle as late as 1814.

The order was soon extended to include the dragoons, who were allowed to keep only one eagle in the field; and in 1809 the Army of Germany was instructed to return all eagles except one per regiment, this one to be carried by the 1st Battalion or 1st Squadron.

The Guard was expanded in 1810–11 to include the 3rd (Dutch) Grenadiers and the 2nd Regiments of Grenadiers and Chasseurs, disbanded in 1808. Each of these new regiments now received one eagle at a parade in the yard of the Tuileries on 15 August 1811. An investigation of the number of eagles present in the regiments of the army at this time yielded a total of 531 eagles still being carried.

On 25 December 1811 an official decree was issued which stated in Article II: 'The eagle is only granted to the Infantry Corps having over 1200 effectives, or to the Cavalry Corps of not less than 600 horses.' This had the effect of officially reducing all infantry and cavalry regiments to one eagle apiece, and in April 1812 all regiments were ordered to return their extra eagles to the Ministry of War in Paris. In fact some regiments ignored the order.

Sometime in 1811 a hollow eagle was made by Thomire and when in 1812 the heavy, embroidered colours and standards were issued (see below) there is some indication that a number of these hollow eagles were produced, although perhaps not issued. They lacked the beautiful workmanship of the 1804 model but must have made the eagle bearers' role easier.

Early in 1813 the cavalry regiments in Spain were ordered to return all their eagles to Paris, and the Line Infantry regiments were reduced to one eagle per brigade, carried by the senior regiment. By now only a few heavy cavalry regiments carried their eagle on campaign, and in the Guard cavalry only the Horse Grenadiers and Chasseurs à Cheval carried them in the field.

3. France: The 8ᵉ Ligne's eagle with wreath, taken by the British 87th Foot in Spain. The wreaths were to be presented by the city of Paris to those regiments involved in the Austerlitz campaign, and 378 were made. The first nineteen were presented on 25 November 1807 to the Guard, and a further 39 were issued in 1808. In 1811 the remainder were still in the Hotel de Ville, Paris, but their subsequent history is unknown, and the only surviving evidence of their appearance is this sketch made by Lt Pym of the 87th.

Most of these eagles were destroyed by order of the Royal Government on the restoration of the monarchy in 1814, and few survived this destruction. When Napoleon returned from Elba, therefore, it was necessary for new eagles to be rapidly manufactured and as a result the eagles of 1815 were of a simplified style with less chisel work. Basically, however, the eagle was as the 1804 model, but with a more tightly crouched stance and a closed beak, and the regimental number now appeared only on the front of the plinth. The eagles of the Guard bore GARDE IMPERIALE instead of a number or badge. The eagles still consisted of six pieces and weighed approximately the same as in 1804. The first presentation of these eagles was made on 1 June 1815 at the Champ de Mai, when 206 eagles were issued: eight to the Guard, 132 to the Infantry, and sixty-six to the Cavalry. Regiments received one eagle, carried on a blue stave as before. The Guard Infantry received only two eagles; one each to the 1st Regiments of Grenadiers and Chasseurs. On 4th June a further eighty-six eagles were issued to the National Guard.

Napoleon ordered that the eagles of all regiments should be carried on the Belgian campaign. However, some regiments carried not the eagles just issued but old eagles which had been preserved and had a far greater value for the men. Regiments which are known to have carried 1804 model eagles in 1815 include the 7th, 8th, 29th and 93rd Line Infantry, 7th Cuirassiers, 5th Chevaux-leger-lanciers, and 3rd and 7th Hussars, the last having the eagle of the 23rd Chasseurs à Cheval, commanded by Colonel Marbot, who was given command of the 7th Hussars in 1815.

In September 1815 ninety-three eagles were delivered to the Arsenal de Bourges and destroyed, together with their flags. In France there remain today fifty-nine of the 1804 eagles, three of 1811, and twelve of the 1815 model. Some sixty eagles have survived in other countries, though few of these were taken in battle: for example, only three were lost in the Russian campaign of 1812, two or possibly three at Leipzig, and two at Waterloo.

When the first eagles were ordered in 1804, new flags were designed to be carried on the staves. In keeping with the superior importance of the eagles, these new flags were of simple design, painted on a single layer of silk, without fringe, cravat or cords. (As usual, exceptions occurred, and it is known that in 1806 the 21st Dragoons adopted cravats thickly embroidered in gold, and carried these until at least 1813. Other regiments may also have adopted such unofficial extras.)

Each battalion and squadron received one of

4. **France: Guidon of the Chasseurs à Cheval de la Garde, 1805–13. (Note: throughout illustrations, only black has been shaded solid, all other colours being left unshaded and described in the body of the text.)**

these new flags, which were 80cm square for infantry, 60cm square for cavalry, and in a swallow-tailed guidon form, 60 by 70cm, for dragoons and horse artillery. In the centre of both faces was a white diamond, surrounded by four corner triangles; on the obverse and reverse these were blue at the top next to the stave and at the bottom of the fly, the other two corners being red (see Plate A1). For Line regiments the obverse bore on the white diamond the dedication L'EMPEREUR/DES FRANCAIS/AU me RÉGIMENT/D'INFANTERIE/DE LIGNE (or LÉGÈRE), cavalry regiments bearing their respective titles in the bottom two lines. The central diamond on the reverse bore VALEUR/ET DISCIPLINE/ me BATAIL- LON (or ESCADRON). The corner wreaths on both sides bore the regimental number.

The flags of the Guard differed in that the white diamond on the reverse bore an Imperial eagle, in a slightly different posture for each corps, with the inscriptions on either side of it: VALEUR . . . . .ET DISCIPLINE and below it me BATAILLON. On the obverse the inscription ended DE LA GARDE/IMPERIALE. At this time there was only one regiment of Grenadiers and one of Chasseurs and their titles were therefore 'Au Régiment de Grenadiers' and 'Au Régiment de Chasseurs'. The eagle on the reverse of the flag of the Marins de la Garde (issued in 1809) was superimposed over an anchor. Each corps of the Guard also carried in the corner wreaths of its flags the appropriate badge instead of a number, i.e. a grenade for the Grenadiers, a bugle horn for the Chasseurs, and an anchor for the Marines. (The eagles and flags of the 2nd Battalions of the Grenadier and Chasseur Regiments were probably used by the 1st Battalions of the 2nd Regiments of those corps raised in April 1806 and disbanded in October 1808.)

The flags of both Line and Guard regiments were carried on the blue stave mentioned previously.

The Guard was expanded in 1810–11 and eagles were presented to the new regiments in August 1811. New flags of a different design were presented to the Guard regiments at the same time, partly because the old flags were showing signs of wear, partly because the introduction of new regiments necessitated changes to regimental titles. These new flags were basically of the 1804 pattern but now bore the regimental number within the corner

wreaths, and the eagle disappeared from the reverse. The dedications now read: obverse, GARDE/IMPERIALE/L'EMPEREUR/DES FRANCAIS/AU er RÉGIMENT/DES GRENADIERS/À PIED (or other regimental title); reverse, VALEUR/ ET DISCIPLINE/ er BATAILLON (or ESCADRON.)

In 1811, when plans had already been made to withdraw the majority of eagles from the regiments, a new pattern of flag was recommended which was to be the exact opposite of the simple 1804 model and, as if to compensate for the loss of eagles, would not only be of the finest silk, richly embroidered with gold wire, but would also sport gold cords, gold fringes on all four sides, and have a velvet cravat, 92cm long by 16cm wide with gold fringes. In the words of Napoleon, 'Price is immaterial.' The decree of 25 December 1811, by which the regiments lost most of their eagles, laid down the specification for these flags and mentioned that henceforth battle honours would be carried on the reverse of the flags. This was a revolutionary step in the design of flags, although an isolated example of a battle honour being carried on a French flag had occurred in the mid-18th century (Régiment de Couronne); and in 1809 the 84th Line had been ordered to carry UN CONTRE DIX on its flags and on plates beneath its eagles in honour of the battle of St Leonard, near Graz, when two battalions of the regiment had held off 10,000 Austrians for fourteen hours. (Two small lines of script on the eagle plates, below UN CONTRE DIX, read 'Devise accordée par L'Empereur/combat de S.Léonard-sous-Graz/25 et 26 juin 1809.'

The design of the 1804 pattern had prevented Napoleon carrying out this idea of battle honours on flags (which he had first introduced in his Army of Italy), but in early 1812 new flags were designed, based on the tricolour, which enabled battle honours to be displayed: see Plate A2. The new flags were ordered on 10th February and the first were delivered to Line regiments in April. Each regiment received one flag, the battle honours restricted to those battles at which Napoleon had commanded in person, i.e. Ulm, Austerlitz, Jéna, Eylau, Friedland, Eckmühl, Essling and Wagram. The battle honours each regiment was entitled to carry up to this date are listed in the following tables (after Hollander):

Infanterie de ligne.
Régiment

1er	Wagram.
2e	Eckmühl, Essling, Wagram.
3e	Ulm, Austerlitz, Jéna, Friedland, Eckmühl, Essling, Wagram.
4e	Ulm, Austerlitz, Jéna, Eylau, Eckmühl, Essling, Wagram.
5e	Wagram.
8e	Austerlitz, Jéna, Friedland, Essling, Wagram.
9e	Wagram.
11e	Ulm, Wagram.
12e	Austerlitz, Jéna, Eylau, Eckmühl, Wagram.
13e	Wagram.
14e	Ulm, Austerlitz, Jéna, Eylau.
15e	Friedland.
16e	Eckmühl, Essling, Wagram.
17e	Austerlitz, Jéna, Eylau, Eckmühl, Wagram.
18e	Ulm, Austerlitz, Jéna, Eylau, Eckmühl, Essling, Wagram.
19e	Wagram.
21e	Austerlitz, Jéna, Eylau, Eckmühl, Wagram.
23e	Wagram.
24e	Jéna, Eylau, Friedland, Essling, Wagram.
25e	Austerlitz, Jéna, Eylau, Eckmühl, Wagram.
27e	Ulm, Jéna, Eylau, Friedland, Essling, Wagram.
28e	Ulm, Austerlitz, Jéna, Eylau.
29e	Wagram.
30e	Austerlitz, Jéna, Eylau, Eckmühl, Wagram.
32e	Ulm, Friedland.
33e	Austerlitz, Jéna, Eylau, Eckmühl, Wagram.
34e	Ulm, Austerlitz.
35e	Ulm, Wagram.
36e	Ulm, Austerlitz, Jéna, Eylau.
37e	Eckmühl, Essling, Wagram.
39e	Ulm, Jéna, Eylau, Friedland, Essling, Wagram.
40e	Ulm, Austerlitz, Wagram.
42e	Wagram.
43e	Ulm, Austerlitz, Jéna, Eylau.
44e	Jéna, Eylau.
45e	Austerlitz, Jéna, Friedland, Essling, Wagram.
46e	Ulm, Austerlitz, Jéna, Eylau, Eckmühl, Essling, Wagram.
48e	Austerlitz, Jéna, Eylau, Eckmühl, Wagram.
50e	Ulm, Jéna, Eylau, Friedland.
51e	Austerlitz, Jéna, Eylau.
52e	Wagram.
53e	Wagram.
54e	Austerlitz, Jéna, Friedland, Essling, Wagram.
55e	Ulm, Austerlitz, Jéna, Eylau.
56e	Eckmühl, Essling, Wagram.
57e	Ulm, Austerlitz, Jéna, Eylau, Eckmühl, Essling, Wagram.
58e	Ulm, Friedland.
59e	Ulm, Jéna, Eylau, Friedland, Essling, Wagram.
60e	Wagram.
61e	Austerlitz, Jéna, Eylau, Eckmühl, Wagram.
62e	Wagram.
63e	Jéna, Eylau, Friedland, Essling, Wagram.
64e	Ulm, Austerlitz, Essling, Wagram.
65e	Eckmühl.
67e	Eckmühl, Essling, Wagram.
69e	Ulm, Jéna, Eylau, Friedland, Essling, Wagram.
72e	Friedland, Eckmühl, Essling, Wagram.
75e	Ulm, Austerlitz, Jéna, Eylau.
76e	Ulm, Jéna, Eylau, Friedland, Essling, Wagram.
79e	Wagram.
81e	Wagram.
84e	Ulm, Wagram.
85e	Austerlitz, Jéna, Eylau, Eckmühl, Wagram.
88e	Ulm, Austerlitz, Essling, Wagram.
92e	Ulm, Wagram.
93e	Eckmühl, Essling, Wagram.
94e	Austerlitz, Jéna, Friedland, Essling, Wagram.
95e	Austerlitz, Jéna, Friedland, Essling, Wagram.
96e	Ulm, Friedland, Essling, Wagram.
100e	Ulm, Essling, Wagram.
102e	Wagram.
103e	Ulm, Essling, Wagram.
105e	Jéna, Eylau, Eckmühl, Essling, Wagram.
106e	Wagram.
108e	Austerlitz, Jéna, Eylau, Eckmühl, Wagram.
111e	Austerlitz, Jéna, Eylau, Eckmühl, Wagram.
112e	Wagram.

The 6th, 7th, 10th, 22nd, 26th, 47th, 66th, 70th, 82nd, 86th and 101st Regiments had no battle honours on their flags: the 31st, 38th, 41st, 49th, 68th, 71st, 73rd, 74th, 77th, 78th, 80th, 83rd, 87th, 89th, 90th, 91st, 97th, 98th, 99th, 104th, 107th, 109th and 110th Regiments' numbers were vacant in 1812.

Infanterie légère.
Régiment

2e	Friedland.
3e	Eckmühl, Essling, Wagram.
4e	Ulm, Friedland.
5e	Wagram.
6e	Ulm, Jéna, Eylau, Friedland, Essling, Wagram.
7e	Jéna, Eylau, Eckmühl, Wagram.
8e	Wagram.
9e	Ulm, Friedland, Essling, Wagram.
10e	Ulm, Austerlitz, Jéna, Eylau, Eckmühl, Essling, Wagram.
12e	Friedland.
13e	Austerlitz, Jéna, Eylau, Eckmühl, Wagram.
15e	Austerlitz, Eckmühl, Wagram.
16e	Jéna, Eylau, Friedland, Essling, Wagram.
17e	Ulm, Austerlitz, Essling, Wagram.
18e	Ulm, Wagram.
21e	Essling, Wagram.
23e	Wagram.
24e	Ulm, Austerlitz, Jéna, Eylau, Eckmühl, Essling, Wagram.
25e	Ulm, Jéna, Eylau, Friedland, Essling, Wagram.
26e	Ulm, Austerlitz, Jéna, Eylau, Eckmühl, Essling, Wagram.
27e	Austerlitz, Jéna, Friedland, Essling, Wagram.
28e	Essling, Wagram.

The 1st, 14th, 19th, 22nd, 31st and 32nd Regiments had no battle honours on their flags: numbers 11, 20, 29 and 30 were vacant in 1812.

Hussards.
Régiment

1er	Ulm, Jéna, Eylau, Friedland.
2e	Austerlitz, Jéna, Friedland.
3e	Ulm, Jéna, Eylau, Friedland.
4e	Austerlitz, Jéna, Friedland.
5e	Austerlitz, Jéna, Eylau, Wagram.
6e	Ulm, Wagram.
7e	Jéna, Eylau, Friedland, Wagram.
8e	Ulm, Austerlitz, Jéna, Eylau, Essling, Wagram.
9e	Ulm, Austerlitz, Friedland, Essling
10e	Ulm, Austerlitz.

Chasseurs à cheval.
Régiment

1er	Austerlitz, Jéna, Eylau, Eckmühl, Wagram.
2e	Austerlitz, Jéna, Eylau, Eckmühl, Wagram.
3e	Friedland, Eckmühl, Wagram.
5e	Austerlitz, Friedland.
6e	Wagram.
7e	Jéna, Eylau, Friedland, Essling.
8e	Ulm, Wagram.
9e	Wagram.
10e	Ulm, Jéna, Eylau, Friedland.
11e	Ulm, Austerlitz, Jéna, Eylau, Friedland, Eckmühl, Wagram.
12e	Austerlitz, Jéna, Eylau, Eckmühl, Wagram.
13e	Ulm, Austerlitz, Eylau, Friedland, Essling, Wagram.
14e	Eckmühl, Wagram.
15e	Friedland.
16e	Austerlitz, Jéna, Eylau, Eckmühl, Essling, Wagram.
19e	Eckmühl, Wagram.
20e	Jéna, Eylau, Friedland, Essling.
21e	Ulm.
22e	Ulm, Austerlitz, Jéna, Eylau, Friedland.
23e	Eckmühl, Essling, Wagram.
24e	Friedland, Essling, Wagram.
26e	Ulm, Austerlitz.

The 4th, 25th and 27th Regiments did not have battle honours; numbers 17 and 18 were vacant in 1812.

Dragons.
Régiment

1er	Ulm, Austerlitz, Jéna, Eylau, Friedland.
2e	Ulm, Austerlitz, Jéna, Eylau, Friedland.
3e	Ulm, Austerlitz, Jéna, Eylau, Friedland.
4e	Ulm, Austerlitz, Jéna, Eylau, Friedland.
5e	Ulm, Austerlitz, Jéna, Eylau.
6e	Ulm, Austerlitz, Jéna, Eylau, Friedland.
8e	Ulm, Austerlitz, Jéna, Eylau.
9e	Ulm, Austerlitz, Jéna, Eylau.
10e	Ulm, Austerlitz, Jéna, Eylau, Friedland.
11e	Ulm, Austerlitz, Jéna, Eylau, Friedland.
12e	Ulm, Austerlitz, Jéna, Eylau.
13e	Ulm, Austerlitz, Jéna, Eylau.
14e	Ulm, Austerlitz, Jéna, Eylau, Friedland.
15e	Ulm, Austerlitz, Jéna, Eylau.
16e	Ulm, Austerlitz, Jéna, Eylau.

17e	Ulm, Austerlitz, Jéna, Friedland.
18e	Ulm, Austerlitz, Jéna, Friedland.
19e	Ulm, Austerlitz, Jéna, Friedland.
20e	Ulm, Austerlitz, Jéna, Eylau, Friedland.
21e	Ulm, Jéna, Eylau.
22e	Ulm, Austerlitz, Jéna, Eylau.
23e	Wagram.
24e	Wagram.
25e	Ulm, Austerlitz, Jéna, Eylau.
26e	Ulm, Austerlitz, Jéna, Eylau, Friedland.
27e	Ulm, Austerlitz, Jéna, Friedland.
28e	Wagram.
29e	Wagram.

The 7th and 30th Regiments had no battle honours.

Carabiniers.
Régiments

1er et 2e	Austerlitz, Jéna, Eylau, Friedland, Eckmühl, Wagram.

Cuirassiers.
Régiment

1er	Ulm, Austerlitz, Jéna, Eylau, Eckmühl, Essling, Wagram.
2e	Austerlitz, Jéna, Eylau, Friedland, Eckmühl, Wagram.
3e	Austerlitz, Jéna, Eylau, Friedland, Eckmühl, Essling, Wagram.
4e	Essling, Wagram.
5e	Ulm, Austerlitz, Jéna, Eylau, Eckmühl, Essling, Wagram.
6e	Essling, Wagram.
7e	Essling, Wagram.
8e	Essling, Wagram.
9e	Austerlitz, Jéna, Eylau, Friedland, Eckmühl, Wagram.
10e	Ulm, Austerlitz, Jéna, Eylau, Eckmühl, Essling, Wagram.
11e	Ulm, Austerlitz, Jéna, Eylau, Eckmühl, Essling, Wagram.
12e	Ulm, Jéna, Eylau, Friedland, Eckmühl, Essling, Wagram.

The battle honours appeared mostly in the central white stripe of the reverse, though the letters encroached on the blue and red sections where two honours were placed in one line. The obverse now bore L'EMPEREUR/NAPOLÉON/AU me RÉGIMENT/ etc. instead of L'EMPEREUR DES FRANCAIS. All inscriptions were in gold.

The Grande Armée departed for the Russian campaign before all the new flags were issued, and the Ministry of War forwarded many of the new flags to the regiments in the field, where they were simply secured to the eagles' staves in place of the old ones. It is possible some regiments either did not receive their new flags or chose to continue to use their old ones, and some 1804 pattern flags may have been carried during the campaign.

None of the Guard regiments were issued with new flags, but carried their 1811 ones until 1813.

5. France: The eagle carried by units on Elba, after Fallou.

New flags were presented to the regiments (one per regiment) with their eagles on 1 July 1815. These flags were again of tricolour design but lacked the fine embroidery of the 1812 pattern due to the speed of manufacture. Only a single line of gold laurel leaves decorated the border, and the inscriptions consisted of letters embroidered in gold on black fabric and sewn to the double layer of silk forming the flag. The red and blue of the tricolour were a pale colour and the size was much larger for infantry than the 1812 issue: 120cm square. Cavalry standards were 55cm square and, because the laurel leaf border was of the same size as on the infantry flags, appeared to be more decorative. For the first time, dragoons also carried standards instead of guidons. The cords were gold and the cravat blue, white and red, with gold fringes. Both were of the same proportions as the 1812 pattern. Cavalry standards had gold fringes on all four edges. The obverse bore L'EMPEREUR/ NAPOLÉON / AU ᵐᵉ RÉGIMENT/ and the corps designation, i.e. Line Infantry, Légère, Hussars etc. The reverse bore the battle honours as listed above but with the addition of those gained in the later campaigns.

The National Guard regiments received flags of the 1812 pattern but with all embroidery in silver instead of gold.

The 1st Grenadiers and 1st Chasseurs de la Garde received two flags with their eagles on 1 June but both were destroyed, and of the Guard's 1815 flags only that of the Horse Artillery survives. We have perforce to assume that flags of a similar pattern were carried by the other regiments. The Horse Artillery's standard follows the 1812 pattern basically in decoration, is 80cm square, and bears the letter N in the wreaths on both sides. However, there is no dedication to the Emperor or unit designation on the obverse; instead there appear the battle honours MARENGO, ULM / AUSTERLITZ, JÉNA / EYLAU, FRIEDLAND / WAGRAM / LA MOSKOWA / LUTZEN, MONTMIRAIL. On the reverse appear VIENNE / BERLIN, MADRID / MILAN, MOSCOU / WARSOVIE / VENISE / LE CAIRE. These are all city names and are out of historical sequence if meant to represent more battle honours. Unfortunately it can only be assumed that other Guard flags followed this design, and it is doubtful if the 1812 model as such was carried.

This was probably because their flags were of such recent issue. The new flags were presented in 1813 at the scale of one per regiment and were of the 1812 Line pattern except the wreaths at the top and bottom (on the white section) carried the corps badge instead of the letter N and on the obverse the inscription began GARDE/IMPERIALE. On the reverse were the honours (the same for all Guard regiments) MARENGO, ULM/AUSTERLITZ, JÉNA / EYLAU, FRIEDLAND / ECKMÜHL, ESSLING/ WAGRAM, SMOLENSK / MOSKOWA / VIENNE, BERLIN / MADRID, MOSCOU. The 1813 flags of the 1st and 2nd Grenadier Regiments survive: both had fringes 25mm wide and embroidered cravats 120cm long.

When Napoleon was banished to Elba in 1814 he was accompanied by a battalion of 608 grenadiers and chasseurs of the Old Guard: the Bataillon Napoléon. They carried an 80cm square white flag with a crimson bend bearing three gold bees and with the words BATAILLON (top of the fly) and NAPOLÉON (bottom, next to the stave) in crimson. The stave was painted with crimson and white spirals and may originally have had a gilt spearhead finial, though Fallou shows a special eagle (see Fig 5). The cords were gold, the cravat crimson and white, embroidered and fringed gold.

Baden

Baden was allied with France in 1805 and in 1806 joined the Confederation of the Rhine, at which time the army consisted of the Gardes du Corps, regiments of light dragoons and hussars, a corps of artillery, and four regiments of infantry, the 1st being the Leibregiment. The infantry was re-organised in 1808 but it is most likely that the new 3rd and 4th Regiments carried the regimental flags of the old regiments of the same number.

From 1805–08 each infantry regiment had two flags, a Leibfahne and a Regimenterfahne. Those carried by the Leibregiment are illustrated in Fig 6. The field was red with a yellow Maltese cross over it, separated from the field by a thin gold braid. Ornament was all gold with a red cross beneath the chain, the arms of Baden being Or, a bend Gules. The field for the central cypher on the reverse was

light blue, the wreath green with blue ribbons. All crowns had a red inner cap and ermine bottom edge. There is some doubt as to the accuracy of this design, as it is based on a flag repaired some time after 1815, but it does seem logical that the Leibregiment's flags would be slightly different to those of the other infantry regiments.

The other infantry regiments bore flags of a common pattern (see Plate D1) with the regiments identified by various colour differences. Thus the Leibfahnen (carried by the 1st Battalions) were in the regimental colour (red for 2nd, dark blue for 3rd, yellow for 4th) with a white cross overall: the Regimenterfahnen (carried by the 2nd Battalions) were white with crosses in the regimental colour. The 4th Regiment had gold wreaths round the cyphers. The reverse of all flags was exactly the same as the obverse. The Leibfahnen were withdrawn in 1808, except possibly from the 2nd Regiment.

Throughout the 1805–15 period these flags were

6. Baden: Pattern for the flags of the Leibregiment from 1805.

11

7. **Baden:** Vexillum carried by the
Garde du Corps.

carried on unpainted staves with brass finials of the pattern illustrated.

The Gardes du Corps had a vexillum, as illustrated in Fig 7. The cloth was almost certainly light blue with silver fringe, cords, chains and finial. The stave and horizontal bar were white. The black griffin, with silver beak, claws and crown, stands on a green mount, holds a shield bearing the arms of Baden, and is surrounded by flags, drums and arms in their natural colours.

The Hussar Regiment carried a white standard of the design illustrated in Fig 8. The arms in the centre are: 1 Checky of red and white: 2 a red rose on white over a black boar on a green mount on yellow field: 3 red lion on white: 4 red, a white bend bearing three black chevrons: 5 a red bend on yellow: 6 a white wing on blue: 7 a red lion issuing from blue wavy lines on a yellow field: 8 yellow, a fess red, and a blue lion on yellow: 9 checky of blue and yellow. The stave was yellow ochre with a gilt finial. The Light Dragoon Regiment's standard is illustrated by Plate D2.

8. Baden: Standard of the Baden Hussar Regiment.

Bavaria

A great number of changes were made to the flags carried by Bavarian regiments during the Napoleonic Wars, and at any one time the flags carried by the army might have included ones dating from the previous century; more recent flags which had been altered as the status and territory of Bavaria changed; or new issues. Records of which regiment carried which type and when are incomplete and it is only possible to list the various types in use during the 1804–15 period, without attributing them to particular regiments. It is known that as late as the 1812 campaign regiments carried flags of *all* the patterns described below.

In 1786, following the unification of the electorates of Bavaria and the Palatinate, new flags were designed, and these were issued to the infantry regiments in 1788. The Leibfahne was as illustrated by Fig 9. The border was in the light blue and white colours of Bavaria, the central field white with the

10. Bavaria: 1803 pattern for Leib- and Ordinärfahnen.

9. Bavaria: 1786 pattern Leibfahne.

Virgin (blue gown over red undergarment) and Child with yellow stars and halo, standing on a blue globe and yellow crescent amongst greyish cloud. The scroll was white with yellow lettering. The reverse bore the arms of Pfalz-Bayern with rampant lion supporters, and beneath it the chains and crosses of the order of the Golden Fleece, the Order of St Hubert, the Order of the Lion of the Palatinate, and the Order of St George. The coat was as follows: gold wheel on red field for Duchy of Cleve: black lion rampant on gold field for Duchy of Jülich: red lion rampant on white field for Duchy of Berg: horizontal black bar on gold field for County of Mors: in the central position, quartered, gold lions rampant on black, and light blue and white lozengy with central red shield bearing gold orb for the Electorate of Bavaria: three gold saltires on red field over three green hills for County of Bergen op Zoom: checky of six, red and white, for the County of Mark: blue lion rampant on white field for the Principality of Veldenz: checky of red and white for the County of Sponheim: white, three red chevrons for County of Ravensburg. Border as for obverse. The three crowned black ravens' heads on a silver field for the County of Rappolstein were added in 1799.

The new Ordinärfahne (Regimenterfahne) of 1786–88 had both obverse and reverse as for the Leibfahne reverse, but on a light blue field. Both flags were 1.73 metres square.

At this time there was one Leib- and one Ordinärfahne per regiment, the Leibfahne being carried by the 1st Battalion, but in October 1801 this was changed to two Leib- and two Ordinärfahnen. In December 1803 the scale was changed again to one Leib- and three Ordinärfahnen, and in March 1804 to one Leib- and one Ordinärfahne, carried by the 1st and 2nd (field) battalions respectively. Two flags per regiment remained the norm for the remainder of the Napoleonic Wars.

Sometime between 1800 and 1803 the design of both sides of the Ordinärfahne was changed to the pattern illustrated by Fig 10, i.e. the arms of Bavaria only, with a lion supporter. The field remained light blue but the triple row of lozengy for the border was sometimes reduced to two rows or increased to four, the number of rows varying from flag to flag.

In 1803 the Ordinärfahne was changed again to the pattern illustrated by Fig 11, in the light blue

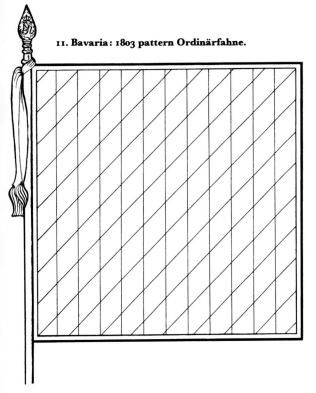

11. Bavaria: 1803 pattern Ordinärfahne.

and white of Bavaria. Ordinärfahnen of this pattern were also issued in 1813 to make good the losses of the 1812 campaign.

The collapse of the Holy Roman Empire caused several Protestant territories to be absorbed by Bavaria and in December 1803 it was decided that the traditional Virgin and Child emblem on the Leibfahne should therefore be replaced by the arms as illustrated in Fig 10, on a white field. From 1803 many regiments either carried Leibfahne and Ordinärfahne of identical patterns (as Fig 10) but with a white and light blue field respectively, or a Leibfahne of this pattern and an Ordinärfahne as shown in Fig 11. In 1806, when Bavaria became a kingdom, the electoral cap over the arms was replaced by a crown, and in July 1808 the arms themselves were changed to create flags of the pattern illustrated in Plate D3. This pattern was also issued in 1813 to regiments which had lost their flags in Russia.

All flags issued before 1813 were carried on staves with a light blue velvet covering: flags issued in 1813 had staves covered in black leather. All staves had a gilt spear-head shaped finial which was either engraved or pierced with the cypher of the elector or king: until 1799 this was CT; 1799–1806 MJ; 1806–15 MJK. Ferrules were also gilt. Blue and white cravats 1.06 metres long by 18cm wide were tied beneath the finial. These cravats usually had gold fringes but were otherwise plain. However, commanders or colonels-in-chief sometimes presented cravats which were richly embroidered with the initials of the donor, or his family arms, or a patriotic slogan, such as STREITTEL UND SIEGET FÜRS VATERLAND (Fight and Conquer for the Fatherland.)

The cavalry regiments carried standards which dated back to the early 1740s. These bore on one side the double-headed eagle of the Holy Roman Empire and on the reverse the arms as illustrated in Fig 10. Each regiment carried, from March 1804, one Leibstandarte, which had a white field. Chevauleger regiments did not carry standards. The two regiments of dragoons converted to chevauleger regiments in 1811 handed in their standards at that time.

In 1814 three new heavy cavalry regiments were raised, the Garde du Corps and 1st and 2nd Kürassiers. Each of these regiments received a white Leibstandarte with gold embroidery and fringes, and two Divisionsstandarten (a division being two squadrons) of light blue, the 2nd Division having silver embroidery, the 3rd gold. These standards were between 40 and 45cm square with gold cords and plain light blue and white cravats with silver fringes. The staves were ribbed, painted light blue, and carried the same type of finial as the infantry.

The reverse of the Kürassier standarte is shown in Plate D4; the obverse was the crest as shown in Plate D3 with the same laurel branches and border details as the reverse of the standarte. The central medallions were of silver with edging and cypher in gold for the Leibstandarten, of gold with edging and cypher in silver for the Ordinärstandarten. The Garde du Corps standarten had oak leaves all round the edges but otherwise followed the same design as those of the Kürassiers.

Saxony

Embroidered flags were issued to the Leib-Grenadier-Garde and twelve Line Infantry regiments of the Saxon army in September 1802 to replace painted ones issued in 1785. Each regiment received a Leibfahne, carried by the 1st Battalion,

and an Ordinärfahne, carried by the 2nd Battalion. These flags were 157cm by 144.5cm. The Ordinärfahne was in the regimental facing colour with a border design as listed in the table below; the Leibfahne white with the same design of border in the regimental facing colour.

The obverse for all flags bore the centre design illustrated in Fig 17, consisting of the quartered arms of Poland (Gules, a spread-eagle Argent crowned, beaked and legged Or) and Lithuania (Gules, a mounted knight and horse Argent, the knight bearing a shield of Azure, a cross Or, and the horse's shabraque Azure edged Or.) Overall was an escutcheon bearing per fess Sable and Argent, two crossed swords Gules, and Barry of ten, Sable and Or, overall a crancelin Vert. These arms were surrounded by gold embroidery and surmounted by a gold crown with a red inner cap, blue and red jewels and white pearls. The reverse of all flags bore the design illustrated in Fig 12: the cypher FA in gold within a gold-edged oval (the colour of the field showing within this border) bordered by gold foliage with red berries, brown stalks, and tied with light blue ribbon edged yellow. At the bottom the star badge and cross of the Military Order of St Friedrich of Saxony; above an elector's cap of crimson and ermine. The four corner shields appeared on the borders of all flags and are the

Saxony			
Regiment	Facing Colour	Border Design	Border Colours
Leib-Gren-Garde	Lemon yellow	13a	Leib: red and green Ordinar: blue and silver-grey
1. Kürfust*	Poppy red	13b	red, yellow, white with green leaves
2. von Sanger	Poppy red	13b	as 1
3. Prinz Anton	Dark Blue	13c	blue and yellow
4. Prinz Clemens	Dark blue	13c	blue and silver
5. Prinz Maximilien	Yellow	13d	yellow and orange with small green leaves
6. von Thümmel	Yellow	13d	orange and silver-grey with dark gold leaves
7. Prinz Friedrich August	Green	13e	Green with brown oak leaves and acorns, yellow flowers
8. von Low	Green	13e	as 7 but white flowers
9. Prinz Xaver**	Light blue	13f	yellow and blue
10. von Bunau†	Light blue	13f	blue and silver
11. von Niesemeuschel	Crimson	13g	poppy red and silver with silver clover leaves
12. von Rechten	Crimson	13g	as 11 but gold clover leaves

* renamed Konig December 1806
** renamed von Oebschelwitz 1807
† renamed von Bevilaqua 1806

crossed swords of Poland described above and the ES cypher for the Elector of Saxony.

These flags were carried on staves of plain wood just under three metres long, with a gilt finial bearing the cypher FA. Cravats and cords do not appear to have been used.

These flags first saw action in the 1806 campaign but the creation of the kingdom of Saxony caused new flags to be ordered in November 1807. The new flags were not ready for the 1809 campaign against Austria and therefore the 1802 flags were carried. The new flags were in fact not presented until July 1811, after the reorganisation of the army, during which the 2nd, 6th, 9th and 10th regiments were disbanded. The two Jäger and two Schützen battalions raised in 1809 were not issued with flags.

As for the 1802 flags, in 1811 each regiment received one Leib- and one Ordinärfahne, both measuring approximately 143cm square, although the length on the stave varied somewhat from flag to flag between 142 and 151cm. The Leibfahne was again white, the Ordinärfahne in the colour of the regiment's facings. Borders remained as listed above, except for the Guard, but the corner shields now bore the arms of Saxony (see Fig 17 and colour

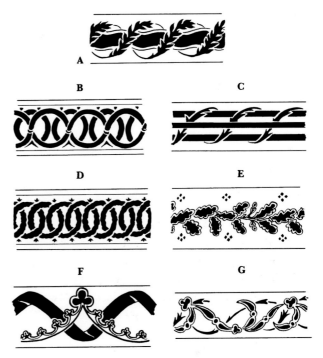

13. Saxony: Border designs for infantry flags.

12. Saxony: Ordinärfahne, 2nd Battalion, Prinz Maximilien Infantry Regiment, 1802–11.

description above.) The border of the Guard's Leibfahne was of the design shown by Fig 13e on a white background and with a red ribbon and green pattern. That of the Ordinärfahne was of the design shown by Fig 13a with a yellow background, the ribbon blue and leaf design in white.

The obverse of all flags now bore in the centre the cypher FAR (as Fig 14) in gold, within the gold outline of a shield, the colour of the field showing within this outline. The shield was surrounded by green foliage and the green ribbon with green, gold edged star of the Order of the Rautenkrone, and surmounted by a crown of gold with red and green jewels. In the centre of the reverse was the Saxon coat of arms (as Fig 15) couched on a red mantle, lined and edged ermine, the ribbons and crown in gold. The Order's crosses and ribbons, and the crown's jewels were as for the obverse. (The red and ermine mantle should have been reserved for the Guard, the Line Infantry's coat of arms having only a surround of green foliage, but the embroiderer erroneously made all flags of the Guard pattern and they were issued without amendment.)

The staves were now in the colour of the regiment's facings; other details as for the 1802 issue. These flags remained in service for the remainder of the Napoleonic Wars, though some

14. Saxony: Central design for the obverse of infantry flags from 1811.

15. Saxony: Central design for the reverse of infantry flags from 1811.

were lost in the 1812 and 1813 campaigns and do not appear to have been replaced.

In 1813 Saxony was occupied by the Allies and a Band of Saxon Volunteers was raised for service against Napoleon. In 1814 these volunteers carried square flags which often bore a Teutonic cross in green or sometimes gold, or occasionally town or family coats of arms and a motto or slogan.

The artillery carried flags of the pattern illustrated by Fig 16. These had been issued in 1753, laid up from 1756–63, reissued in 1763 and carried with the guns in the field until May 1810, when they were laid up for the last time. These flags were white with a blue border; the small grenades in this border were silver with red and yellow flames, the large corner grenades being brown with similar flames. The crown was gold with a red inner cap, blue and red jewels and white pearls. The blue mantle was lined and edged ermine, with gold ribbons, and bore four shields, all edged gold: top centre, blue with a gold AR cypher; left and right, red with the Polish and Lithuanian arms described earlier; bottom, the crossed swords and Saxon arms also described earlier. In the central base is an altar in outline, bearing a gold salamander surrounded by flame, the whole surrounded by a

17. Saxony: Leibstandarte for cavalry regiments, 1785–1810.

Chevauleger Regt Polenz, white border edged gold, light blue arrowheads, gold floral design; 18e Chevauleger Regt Prinz Jean, white border edged gold, mid-blue design with green palm leaves; 18f Chevauleger Regt Prinz Albrecht, white border edged green, brown acorns and twigs, green leaves; 18g Chevauleger Regt Prinz Clemens, white border edged green, green leaf design, purple pear and oval shapes.

The Karabiniers, disbanded in 1810, carried four white standards with a border as illustrated in Fig 19. The border was white, edged gold, with a design of red 'sixes' and 'nines' and green leaves. At the corners the circle was red, enclosing gold studs, cross and saltire, with a green stud at the centre. This illustration shows the reverse for all cavalry standards of this period. The crown is gold, without an inner cap; the cypher is also gold, the leaves green on brown stems. The fringe and cords on this standard are alternate silver and green.

As with the infantry, new standards were ordered late in 1807 but were not presented until July 1811, after the regiments had been re-organised. Regiments were again given four standards, one per squadron, each 71cm square

trophy of arms in natural colours, except the cannon are gold.

The cavalry was issued with standards, with an obverse as illustrated by Fig 17, in 1785 and carried these until 1810. Colour detail is described above, with the fringe, cords and corner cyphers (AR3) all in gold. These standards were 71cm square and were issued four per regiment – one for each squadron. In the heavy cavalry all standards were Leibstandarten and had white fields: in the chevauleger regiments there was one white Leibstandarte and three Ordinärstandarten. Hussar regiments did not have standards.

Squadrons were identified by tying a 56cm cravat below the finial: 1st Squadron white; 2nd red; 3rd blue; 4th yellow. Cords were of the same colour. The stave was of unpainted wood, the gilt finial as illustrated. Regiments were distinguished by the borders only, these borders being in the colours of the regiment's facings and buttons: Fig 18a Garde du Corps, white border with gold edging and design, centre crosses silver; 18b Cuirassiers of the Guard, white border edged gold, design in crimson; 18c Zastrow's Cuirassiers, white border edged gold, leaf design in green, spots gold; 18d

18. Saxony: Border designs for cavalry standards.

19. Saxony: Leibstandarte of the Karabiniers, to 1810.

without the fringe, carried on staves just under three metres long with a brass ferrule and broad-bladed spearhead shaped finial. The stave was ribbed longitudinally and had a steel hand guard.

The Garde du Corps carried standards with the obverse bearing the Saxon arms on a red mantle, lined and edged ermine, surmounted by a gold crown and surrounded by the green ribbon of the Order of the Rautenkroner (see Plate E4). The reverse bore the gold crown and cypher FAR within green branches with brown stems, as illustrated by Fig 19. The border design remained unchanged. The field of every standard was white.

All other cavalry regiments, except the Hussars who did not carry flags, received standards of a similar pattern except on the obverse the Saxon crowned shield was not on a mantle but only flanked by green palm and laurel branches – see Fig 14. All standards of the two cuirassier regiments had white fields; the chevauleger regiments had one white Leibstandarte and three red Ordinärstandarten with white borders. The border designs were as for the previous issue.

The fringes and cords of the standards of the Garde du Corps were sky blue and gold; those of the Leib Cuirassiers and Prinz Johann regiments were scarlet and silver; the Zastrow Cuirassiers had scarlet and silver fringes but yellow and silver cords. The Prinz Clemens chevauleger regiment had fringes and cords of light green and gold; Prinz Albrecht of dark green and gold; and Polenz of light blue and gold.

The Landwehr cavalry raised in 1813–14 carried a variety of standards, most of which, like their infantry counterparts, were white, less often green, and usually bore a gold or green Teutonic cross. Mottoes or unit names were often inscribed round the cross.

Württemberg

Württemberg joined the Confederation of the Rhine in July 1806 and supplied Napoleon with eight (later nine) Line Infantry regiments, two Chevauleger regiments, one Dragoon and one Chasseur à Cheval regiment, as well as Light Infantry, Artillery and a Royal Guard.

20. Württemberg: 1811 pattern for infantry regiments.

The basic pattern of flag carried by all Line Infantry from May 1811 is shown by Fig 20. The size was 132 by 118cm. All had 7cm gold fringes, a gold cypher and crown on the obverse, and on the reverse a coat of arms couched on a red mantle, lined ermine, edged and ribboned gold, and surmounted by a gold crown. The supporters are a brown stag and a black lion, each holding a yellow standard bearing a black eagle. The shield is surmounted by a gold crown and has the gold chains and crosses of the Orders of the Golden Eagle and the Military Order of Württemberg below it. The coat of arms is per pale Or, three antlers Sable: Or, three lions rampant Sable.

These flags were carried on a wooden stave, the top half of which was painted black, with a brass ferrule and a brass finial of the pierced design illustrated. Overall length of the stave, including finial, was 3.08 metres. Each regiment originally had two flags of this pattern (one per battalion), except the 6th Regiment which had four, but by 1814 all regiments had four flags except the 9th, which had two. It is likely that only two flags were carried on campaign by the two field battalions, the other flags remaining at the regimental depot.

The flags of the various regiments were distinguished by the colour of their field: 1st, lemon yellow; 2nd scarlet; 3rd turquoise; 4th rose pink; 5th sky blue; 6th, quarterly, blue and white; 7th, quarterly, blue and scarlet; 8th, quarterly, blue and yellow; 9th dark blue. The Chasseur and Light Infantry battalions did not carry flags.

Of the cavalry only the two chevauleger regiments appear to have carried standards. From 1811 these were of the same pattern as the infantry flags, the two squadron standards of the 1st Regiment having yellow fields and those of the 2nd Regiment having red fields.

Würzburg

The Grand Duchy of Würzburg was created in December 1805 and the Grand Duke Ferdinand (of Tuscany) quickly raised an infantry regiment of two battalions and a dragoon regiment of two squadrons. Both regiments fought for Napoleon in Spain and the 1812 Russian campaign.

The infantry regiment became the 1st Regiment of the Confederation of the Rhine in 1806 and on 8th August that year was presented with four flags of the pattern illustrated by Fig 21. These flags were lemon yellow with a border of alternately red, white and blue dogs' teeth. In the centre of the obverse was the red cypher F surmounted by a gold crown and surrounded by green laurel branches tied with red ribbon. On the reverse the central device was the full coat of arms of the Grand Duchy, couched on a red mantle, lined and edged ermine, surmounted by a gold crown, tied with gold ribbons, the shield surrounded by the gold chains of the Order of the Golden Fleece and the Royal Tuscan Order of San Stefano, the latter bearing a white cross. The shield bore firstly the arms of Würzburg: quarterly 1 and 4 per fess dancetty Gules and Argent, for Franconia; 2 and 3 Azure, a standard quarterly Sable, Argent, Or and Gules on a lance Or, for Würzburg. Secondly the arms of the House of Habsburg-Lothringen: quarterly of eight, 1 Barry of six Gules and Argent, for Hungary Ancient; 2 Gules, a mount Vert bearing a patriarchal cross Argent, for Hungary Modern; 3 and 4 together, Gules, a lion rampant fourchée Argent, crowned Or, for Bohemia; 5 Or, an eagle displayed Sable, crowned Or and bearing on its breast a cross Argent, for Silesia; 6 Or, five torteaux, a sixth Hurt, bearing three fleur-de-lis, for Tuscany; 7 Or, a bend Gules bearing three alerions Argent, for Lorraine; 8 Or, a lion rampant Gules, crowned Azure, for Habsburg. Overall an escutcheon of Austria, Gules, a fess Argent, crowned with a crimson cap and ermine circlet.

These flags were 160 by 120cm and were carried on a stave painted with red and white spirals. Würzburg was embodied in the kingdom of Bavaria in 1814 and the regiment was transferred to the Bavarian army, where it received new flags of the Bavarian pattern.

The dragoon regiment (re-formed as Chevaulegers in 1812) carried a white standard of the pattern illustrated by Fig 22. The borders were gold, the central medallion of the obverse was rose pink (possibly red originally) with gold surround, and the cypher, crown, laurel and other embroidery also in gold. The arms on the reverse were quarterly Franconia and Würzburg, with an escutcheon of Austria. The stave was as for the infantry.

21. Würzburg: 1806 pattern for infantry.

22. Würzburg: 1806 pattern for dragoons.

24

1

2

3

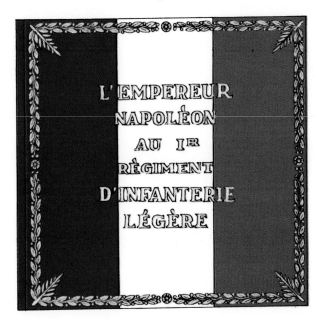

4

1 France: 1804 pattern
2 France: 1812 pattern
3 France: 1815 pattern
4 France: Régiment Irlandais

1

2

3

4

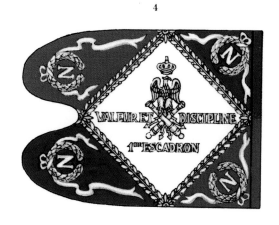

1 France: Régiment d'Elite Gendarmerie à Pied (obverse)
2 France: Régiment d'Elite Gendarmerie à Pied (reverse)
3 France: Marins de la Garde
4 France: Horse Artillery of the Guard

1

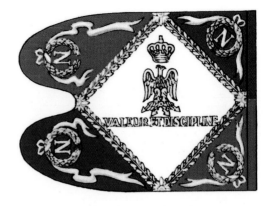

2

3

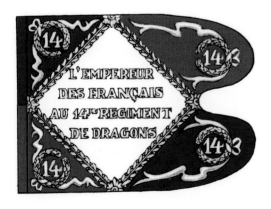

4

1 France: Dragoons of the Guard
2 France: Mameluks of the Guard
3 France: 14th Dragoons
4 France: 11th Chasseurs à Cheval

1

2

3

4

1 **Baden: 3rd Regt of Line Infantry**
2 **Baden: Light Dragoons**
3 **Bavaria: 1808 Infantry pattern**
4 **Bavaria: 1st Kürassier Regt**

D

1

2

3

4

1 Berg: 1809-13 Infantry pattern
2 Hesse-Darmstadt: 1804-12 Leibfahne
3 Saxony: 1810-13 Infantry pattern
4 Saxony: Garde du Corps

1

2

3

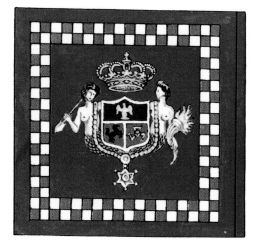

4

1 Westfalia: 1808-13 Infantry pattern
2 Westfalia: 1st Hussars 1812-13
3 Naples: 1811 Infantry pattern
4 Naples: 1806 Infantry pattern

1

2

3

4

1 Italy: Grenadiers of the Royal Guard
2 Italy: 1809 Infantry pattern
3 Italy: Gardes d'Onore
4 Italy: 1st Cacciatori a Cavallo

1

2

3

4

1 **Duchy of Warsaw: 4th Line Infantry**
2 **Duchy of Warsaw: 6th Line Infantry**
3 **Polish Troops: Légion de Vistule**
4 **Polish Troops: Lanciers de Vistule**

In 1814 the two squadrons became the 3rd and 4th Squadrons of the 1st Royal Bavarian Lancers and presumably carried standards of the Bavarian pattern.

Naples

In 1806 the Neapolitan infantry regiments adopted flags of the same basic pattern as those of the French infantry, except the blue triangular corners were black. It is not known why black was chosen, but during the Republic of Naples the Calabrian Legion had black flags, and the provincial legions had always used red and black insignia.

These flags were of the same size as the French ones, 80cm square, but Napoleon forbade the issue of eagles to Neapolitan troops in August 1807 and they were therefore carried on black staves with a brass ferrule and a plain iron finial of spear-head shape. There was one flag per battalion.

Only one flag of this pattern survives, that of the 1st Light Infantry, originally in the collection of the Prince of Moskowa, Paris. It is not known when it was issued. The obverse is shown by Plate F4: the reverse is of the same pattern but in the central diamond bore the arms of the kingdom with an escutcheon of France overall (gold Imperial eagle on a blue shield mounted on a red mantle, lined ermine and fringed gold, with a gold crown over the mantle.) The author has been unable to decypher the arms of the kingdom as shown by Over and in Tradition magazine, and cannot as yet trace them elsewhere. At the top of the arms are the three legs symbol of the Two Sicilies and the black horse of Naples, and in the 4th grand quarter are the arms of Aragon quartered saltirewise with Calabria. The whole is displayed on a blue mantle, lined ermine, with a gold fringe and border of white and amaranth checks. The supporters are the two mermaids as Fig 23 except they both hold spears. The mantle is surmounted by a crown as in Fig 23.

Murat became king in 1808 and Joseph's name was ordered to be removed from the flags and replaced by Gioachino (Murat). However, there is some evidence that the flags were simply withdrawn.

The Guardia Civica Provinciale, formed by Joseph when king, were given new flags of white, with in the centre the arms of the kingdom and (probably on the reverse) the arms of the province to which the Guard belonged. LIBERTA appeared on the obverse, SICUREZZA on the reverse.

Flags were issued to the 3rd and 4th Line Regiments in 1809, and the 1st and 2nd Line Regiments (in Spain) received flags from Murat for a review. However, it is believed these were the flags of Joseph's time, drawn from the stores for review purposes only. Perhaps as a result of this, on 15 February 1811 Murat ordered new flags to be issued. Their basic pattern is illustrated by Fig 23. Colour detail of the reverse may be seen in Plate F3: the chain and cross are of the Order of the Two Sicilies. The obverse had the same field and border colours, with gold crown and inscription, green branches tied with a light blue ribbon.

The inscriptions on the obverse of the flags of the 5th and 6th Regiments were slightly different to the basic style, incorporating the names of the regiments: AL REGG^{to}/REAL/CALABRIA/5° DI LINEA and AL/REGGIMENTO/DI NAPOLI/6° DI LINEA. On the flag of the 7th the inscription read AL 7° REGGIMENTO/FANTERIA/DI LINEA. The 7th had only one battalion in 1813, formed of negroes with officers from Haiti and the French West Indies, and this now had the title Principe Luciano, which appeared at the bottom of the inscription on the obverse from 1813.

The 1811 pattern was carried on a stave painted with white and amaranth spirals and most regiments had a light blue cravat, with gold fringes and sometimes a diced border as on the flags, tied below the finial. The 5th Line had two cravats, green and violet: the 6th Line also had two cravats of white with gold fringes. Cords of gold were now used and the plain finial had been replaced by the prancing horse of Naples on the capital of a Corinthian column, as illustrated by Fig 24. The finial was all gilt.

Ghisi is of the opinion that these 1811 flags were in fact ordered and perhaps issued as early as 1809, and were certainly issued to all regiments by the spring or summer of 1810. He believes that the 1811 order refers only to the naval and civilian flags of the kingdom, which had remained red, white and black as under Joseph. Certainly it seems unlikely that a man such as Murat would have allowed the troops of his kingdom to carry old flags – or no flags – for almost three years.

New flags were issued on 4 November 1814 to the 5th and 6th Line but only that of the 5th has survived. (It was captured by the Russians at Danzig in November 1814.) This flag is 130 by 150cm and of the same basic pattern as the reverse of the 1811 pattern (Plate F3) except the black horse of Naples and the Trinacria of the Two Sicilies are now both on a yellow field. The obverse bears the same coat of arms with above it the inscription ONORE E FEDELTA SENZA MACCHIA (Honour and Fidelity without stain) and below GIOACCHINO MURAT / AL 6° REGGIMENTO / FANTERIA DI LINEA. This flag is red instead of light blue and it is not known whether there has been a chemical alteration in the paint over the years, or whether a red flag was issued to this regiment, perhaps as an honour or indication that the regiment was raised in Naples itself. It is not known if the finial was still in the form of a horse.

The 1814 flag of the Régiment de Grenadiers à pied de la Garde Royale was of the same size and colour with the same border and cravat as Line regiments, except on the reverse ONORE E FEDELTA appeared above the arms, SENZA MACCHIA below, and on the obverse there were no branches or crowned cypher, instead only the inscription in large gold letters: GIOACCHINO NAPOLEONE/AL REGGIMENTO/DI GRANATIERI A PIED/DELLA GUARDIA REALE. The cravat had a checkered pattern near the ends with a gold crown over a letter G, also in gold, above this pattern.

The standards of the cavalry regiments from 1811 (or possibly from 1809) were of the same design as for infantry regiments (see Fig 23) except the inscription on the obverse was different. For the regiments of Chasseurs à Cheval it read: AL ° REGG^to/CACCIATORI/A CAVALLO: for the regiments of Cavalerie Légère it read: AL ° REGG^to/CAVALLEGGIERI. These standards were 45 by 38 cm and were carried until 1813. The standards of the other cavalry regiments are not known.

Italy

The flags of the Italian forces had been influenced by those of the French Army since 1798 and the basic pattern of flag issued to the Line Infantry regiments during the republican period (1802–05) was therefore of a distinctly French style; in fact exactly the same pattern as that used by the French Gendarmerie at this time, but with green replacing blue because of the difference in national colours. This basic pattern is illustrated by Fig 25 and was approved by the Italian War Ministry in May 1802. The corners were red, the central square olive green, the balance gold and the central diamond and small square in the canton (for the unit designation) were white. These flags were carried on a stave painted in spirals of white, red and green, with a spear-head shaped finial. Silver cords, and a long tricoloured cravat with silver fringes, were tied beneath the finial. Cavalry standards were similar but had fringes.

These flags were presented to the regiments as they passed the Tuileries en route to the Channel camps for the invasion of England. Thus on 15 January 1804 Napoleon as First Consul presented flags of this pattern to the 2nd Hussars, the Horse Artillery, and 1st Light Brigade. On 22 January he presented flags to the 1st Infantry Brigade. Other flags were subsequently presented without ceremony, Napoleon now being preoccupied with his plans to become Emperor.

In 1805 the kingdom of Italy was formed, the demi-brigades were converted into regiments (the 1st and 2nd Hussars became the Dragoni Regina, and the Presidential Guard the Royal Guard), and flags of the French Line Infantry pattern of 1804 were ordered, again with green in place of the blue parts. The first formation to receive this new pattern was the Infantry of the Guard, which was garrisoned in Paris for duty at the Imperial Palace. (Brunon states that the regiment received its eagles on 1 September 1806 at the camp of Boulogne). The Grenadiers' flag was 80cm high by 86cm wide and is illustrated by Plate G1. This flag was soon replaced by one with the inscriptions in Italian: NAPOLEONE/IMPERATORE E RE/AL REGGIMENTO GRANATIERI/A PIEDI DELLA GUARDIA/REALI, and on the reverse GUARDIA REALI/VALORI/E DISCIPLINA.

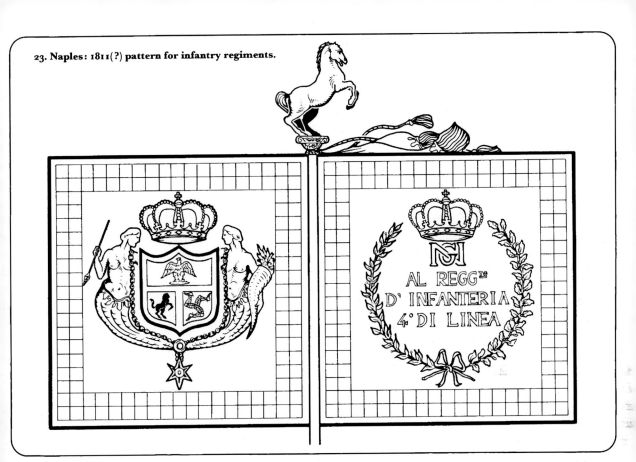

23. Naples: 1811(?) pattern for infantry regiments.

AL REGG.^{to} D' INFANTERIA 4° DI LINEA

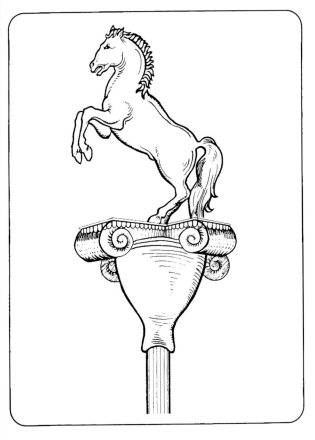

24. Naples: Finial for 1811 pattern.

The Guard Cacciatori (known as Carabinieri from 1810) had a flag of the same pattern but with bugle horns in place of the grenades and laurels in the corners, and CACCIATORI in place of GRANATIERI in the inscription. The Guard Veliti did not carry flags.

The new flags for the Line Infantry were ready for presentation on 13 June 1805 at Montechiari, near Brescia, by the Emperor. These had a lion instead of an eagle on the stave, and it was probably for this reason – the Guard having already received flags and French *eagles* – that the presentation was never made. What followed is not precisely known, but it is almost certain that Line Infantry regiments continued to carry their old republican flags. The staves probably remained painted in white, red and green spirals during this period of transition, with spear-head shaped finials, cravat and cords as described above.

In 1809 the Line Infantry regiments were at last issued with new flags to replace those of the Italian Republic, which had remained in service up to that date. The obverse is illustrated in Plate G2; Fig 26 shows both obverse and reverse. On the reverse the top left and bottom right corners were red, the others green; corner emblems and laurel round the central white diamond were all gold; central arms were green mantle, gold eagle, mantle fringe, crown, chain and cross, with the halberds in proper colours. The star above the eagle was silver. The large shield was red, edged gold, with a gold crown, and the smaller shield light blue with a gold N. The scrolls were light blue and lettering gold.

The stave was probably black now, and topped by a gilt eagle made in Milan by Francesconi's foundry. The eagle was 20cm high, on a plinth 5cm high, and with a 6cm long tube to receive the stave below that. The regimental number was in relief on the front of the plinth. These eagles were not exactly the same as the French ones: they had the head turned towards the eagle's right, and the talons did not lie flat above the Jupiter's spindle. As in the French Army, there was supposedly one eagle per regiment but in fact almost every battalion appears to have carried an eagle above its flag.

A new flag of French pattern was issued in 1813 following the Russian campaign. This was 80cm square, carried on a black stave with the Italian eagle at the top, and with the red and green corners and white central diamond of the earlier flags. The obverse bore in gold on the central diamond the inscription NAPOLEONE/IMPERATORE E RE/AL ^{o} REGGIMENTO/FANTERIA/DI LINEA or LEGGERA for Light Infantry. The Line Infantry flag is illustrated by Fig 27: colours as for the 1808 model. The pattern for the Guard Infantry is illustrated by Fig 28.

During the 1808–13 period the Foot Artillery carried two flags of the infantry pattern but with the inscription NAPOLEONE/IMPERATORE DE FRANCESI / RE D'ITALIA / AL I^{o} REGGIMENTO / D'ARTIGLIERIA in gold on the blue globe. The same inscription was probably carried on the 1813 pattern.

The Horse Artillery carried four standards of the infantry pattern during the 1808–13 period, with the inscription: NAPOLEONE/IMPERATORE E RE/AL 2° REGGIMENTO/D'ARTIGLIERI/A CAVALLO. The corner emblems on the reverse consisted of crossed cannon beneath a gold iron crown and the lettering on the two scrolls was limited to VALORE above the eagle and E DISCIPLINA below it. From 1813 a flag of the Cacciatori a Cavallo pattern was carried (see below).

Dragoons were issued with one standard per squadron but according to Crociani also carried a larger (circa 80cm square) flag of the infantry pattern as a regimental standard, as would befit dragoons. This regimental flag was known as the 'Napoleone'. Both flag and standard followed the 1808–13 infantry pattern, the standards being 60cm square, and were carried on staves topped by an Italian eagle. The 'Napoleone' of the Dragoni Napoleone Regiment has survived and bears on the central globe the inscription: NAPOLEONE/ IMPERATORE DE FRANCESI/RE D'ITALIA/AL REGGIMENTO/DRAGONI/NAPOLEONE. The top scroll bears VALORE E DISCIPLINA, the lower one NEL TUO NOME VITTORIOS (Victorious in your name). There is a gold N in gold laurel wreaths in each corner. Squadron standards were similar but had gold fringes. That of the 4th Squadron of the Regina Regiment has survived. The inscription reads NAPOLEONE / IMPERATORE DE FRANCESI / RE D'ITALIA/AL REGG^{to} DE DRAGONI/DELLA REGINA. A scroll below this bears 4° SQUADRONE. The reverse is as above but a five-pointed silver star replaces the crown over the coat of arms.

In 1813 new standards were issued and the blue globe was omitted, leaving only the laurel and oak leaf wreath within the central diamond. Two examples have survived. The standard of the 2nd Squadron, Dragoni Napoleone is 56cm square and bears in the centre of the obverse DRAGONI NAPOLEONE/ 2° SQUA^{ne}. On the reverse the corner emblems were crowns over the letter N, all in gold (see Guard of Honour flag, Plate G3.) The 1813 squadron standard of the 1st Squadron, Dragoni della Regina bears in the centre of the obverse the inscription NAPOLEONE/IMPERATORE DE FRANCESI/RE D'ITALIA/AL REGG^{to} DE DRAGONI/DELLA REGINA. Above this is a scroll bearing VALORE E DISCIPLINA, and below another scroll bearing I^{o} SQUADRONE. On this particular standard the coloured corners are reversed, being on the obverse red at top left and bottom right, the others green.

Of the standards of the Light Horse regiments (Cacciatori a Cavallo) only two have survived. Both are of the 1813 pattern described for dragoons except the obverse has no oak and laurel wreath round the inscription and the reverse has crowned bugle horns in gold in each corner: see Plate G4. The standard of the 1st Regiment is 60cm square,

without a fringe, and bears the inscription on the obverse NAPOLEONE/IMPERATORE E RE/AL 1º REGGIMENTO/CACCIATORI REALI/A CAVALLO. On the obverse of the standard of the 2nd Regiment is NAPOLEONE/IMPERATORE E RE/AL 2ºREGGᵗᵒ CACCIATORI/A CAVALLO/PRINCIPE REALE. A figure 2 appears inside the bugle horn in each corner of the reverse: the top scroll is as for the 1st Regiment, but the bottom scroll bears 3º SQUAD-RONE. The 60cm square standard was carried on a

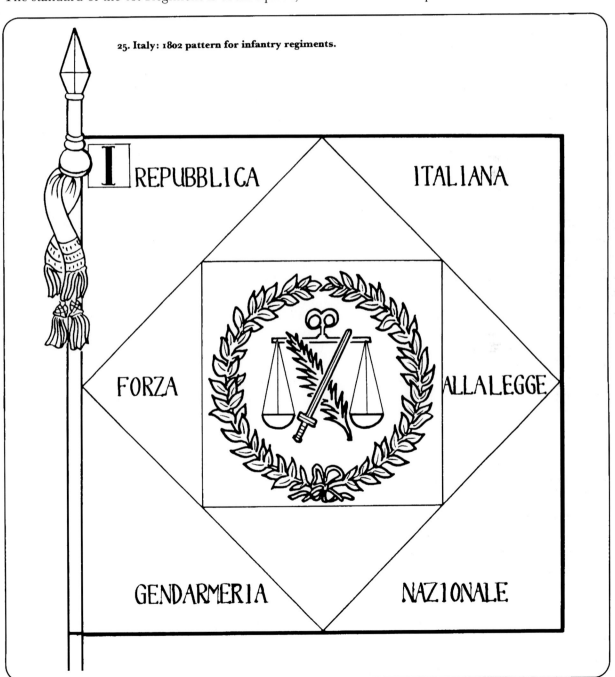

25. Italy: 1802 pattern for infantry regiments.

stave with an eagle bearing the number 2 on its plinth.

The Royal Guard cavalry consisted of three regiments: Dragoni della Guardia, Gendarmeria Scelta, and Guardia d'Onore. The standard of the latter is illustrated by Plate G3. The Dragoni della Guardia bore a 6ocm square standard of the 1808–13 infantry pattern but with a fringe. The obverse bore on the blue globe the inscription NAPOLEONE/IMPERATORE DE FRANCESI/RE D'ITALIA/AL DRAGONI/DELLA GUARDIA/REALE. The blue scroll above the globe bore VALORE E DISCIPLINA, the lower scroll º SQUADRONE. The reverse was as in Fig 26 but without the scrolls, a gold letter N in each corner wreath, and with a gold fringe.

Only one standard of the 1813 issue survives. This is 56cm square and follows the new infantry pattern, with on the obverse the inscription NAPOLEONE/IMPERATORE E RE/AL

DRAGONI/DELLA GUARDIA/REALE. The reverse was of the Cacciatori a Cavallo pattern (Plate G4) but with the letter N within the corner emblems.

The Gendarmeria Scelta della Guardia Reale from 1810 carried the standard illustrated by Fig 29. This was 6ocm square and in the usual colours, except the grenade emblems and fringe were silver.

Polish Troops

By the end of 1806 the newly formed Duchy of Warsaw had an army of some 30,000 men and during January and February 1807 divisions were detached to serve with the French Army. On 3 May, in the Royal Gardens of Warsaw, eagles and flags were distributed to the regiments of the new duchy.

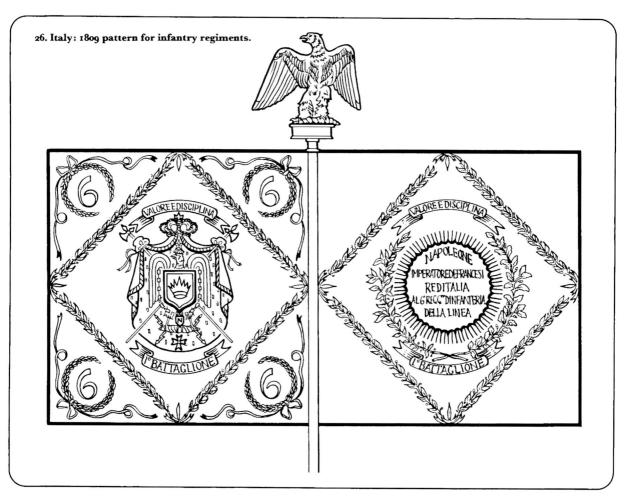

26. Italy: 1809 pattern for infantry regiments.

It is probable that, as in the French Army, each regiment received an eagle to be carried by the 1st Battalion, the other battalions receiving flags without eagles, but, as in the French Army, these regulations were not strictly obeyed and a number of anomalies occur in the surviving flags. Also, unlike the French Army, the Polish regiments appear to have been issued with or adopted eagles which did not follow a uniform pattern and were of various sizes and postures. Two eagles carried by 2nd Battalions have also survived, which suggest that it was not uncommon for battalions other than the 1st to carry eagles.

The Army of the Duchy of Warsaw was relatively small and it is therefore possible to list here all known examples of flags and eagles so that the individual variations may be described. Most of these eagles and flags are preserved in the Notre Dame Cathedral of Kazan and are trophies of the wars of 1812 and 1813, but three flags (of the 4th, 6th and 8th Infantry Regiments) are in the Musee Czartoryski in Cracow, and the flags of the 14th Infantry and fanions of the 1st Regiment of Chevaulegers are in the Swiss museum of Rapperswyl. Information on all these flags and eagles has been taken from Chelminski, Andolenko and Bahrynowski.

1st Regt of Infantry   Eagle: silver with gold crown; white metal plaque below with gold lettering, on the front PULK 1szy (1st Regiment) over PIECHOTY (Infantry): on the rear woysko (Army) over POLSKIE (Polish.) Flag: 94 by 80cm. A white flag with in the centre a silver eagle with a gold crown and the inscription RÉPUBLIQUE FRANCAISE on the obverse, POLSKI LEGION on the reverse. This flag was captured in 1812 and probably dates from before 1807. It was replaced by a crimson flag 55cm square bearing a white eagle in the centre of both sides, with beneath it in yellow PULK PIERWSZY/PIECHOTY.

2nd Regt of Infantry   Flag: 48 by 50cm. Both sides crimson with a silver fringe, a white eagle in the centre, and above the eagle the words PULK 2yc PIECHOTY, and below it LEGIA 1.

4th Regt of Infantry (See Plate H1)   Chelminski describes this regiment's flags as being of crimson silk with a white Polish eagle in the centre, above the eagle the inscription 'Gdy sie chce bronic nie innych ciemiezi/Haslem Polaka rginac lub zwycieczyc'. (To defend ourselves but not oppress others. The slogan of the Polish is to vanquish or die.) Bahrynowski describes a second flag as 42 by 51cm with an 8cm silver fringe. The obverse was crimson (Plate H1), the reverse light blue and bearing the same design as the obverse. On the reverse, about 8cm in from the edge of the fly, and running the full depth of the flag parallel to the fly, was the inscription 'Svte reka Zofii Potocki Zony Oierwszego Polkownika Regimentu'. (Sewn and made by the hand of Sofia Potocki, wife of the first colonel of the regiment.) A 4th Regiment was formed from the remnants of the 4th, 7th and 9th Regiments in 1813 and this may account for there being two different flags.

5th Regt of Infantry   Eagle: silver, 18cm high by 20cm wide, carried on a stave 2.24 metres long. Flag: crimson with a white eagle and silver fringe; inscription above eagle unknown.

6th Regt of Infantry (See Plate H2)   Flag: 54cm by 60cm, of crimson silk with a white eagle; crown, beak, legs, sceptre and orb in gold. Above the eagle in gold is woysko polskie; below, also in gold, PULK SZUSTY. Silver fringe.

7th Regt of Infantry   Eagle: silver with gold crown, 22cm high by 30cm wide. On the front of the plaque beneath the eagle is the inscription PULK 7/PIECHOTY; on the rear woysko/polskie. The 2nd Battalion is believed also to have carried a silver eagle, 23cm by 20.5cm with a blackened iron plaque (8.6cm by 22.6cm and 1.7cm thick) bearing a gilt border and the usual inscription: PULK 7/PIECHOTY; woysko/polskie. Below the plaque was a gilt tube 9cm in length into which fitted a black stave 2.29 metres long with a brass ferrule. Flag: not known but Andolenko shows the eagle and stave with a square French(?) flag attached, as taken at Wiasma in 1812. The flag follows the usual French 1804 pattern but has an Imperial (?) eagle in the central white diamond with a battalion number below, and in the corners bears the bugle horn device enclosing the figure 7. The corner embroidery is silver, as is the battalion number. It is not known if this was in fact the flag of the 7th Polish Regiment.

8th Regt of Infantry Eagle: silver. Flag: 42cm square, crimson with a silver fringe and eagle. Above the eagle is PULK 8szy /PIECHOTY on the obverse; BATTALION 1e on the reverse. All lettering is black.

10th Regt of Infantry Eagle: silver with gold crown, 22cm by 23cm, on a stave 2.92 metres long. On the plaque in gold PULK 10ty/PIECHOTY. There is no information on a flag but a cravat of white silk, 53cm long, was tied beneath the eagle. The cravat had gold oak and laurel leaves embroidered along the edges and had gold fringes.

11th Regt of Infantry Eagle: silver, 21.5cm high by 20cm wide. Plaque PULK 11ty/PIECHOTY on the obverse, WOYSKO/POLSKIE on the reverse. Again no information on a flag, but a plain white cravat 62cm long by 6cm wide, with gold fringes, was tied beneath the eagle.

13th Regt of Infantry (See Fig 30) Eagle: white metal with gold crown, 22cm high by 20cm wide. Plaque inscription, the reverse of the usual, reads on the obverse WOYSKO / POLSKIE, on the reverse PULK 13/PIECHOTY. A white cravat, 62cm long by 15cm wide, embroidered with small silver stars and with a silver fringe, was tied below the eagle. The 2nd Battalion also carried a silver eagle, without a crown. The silver plaque was edged gold and had the usual inscription, also in gold, but in one line, i.e. obverse PULK 13 PIECHOTY; reverse WOYSKO POLSKIE. Flag: the flag of the 2nd Battalion survives, see Fig 30. Size 65cm by 69cm, fringe 4cm wide. The flag was white with a gold fringe, inner borders and laurel leaves of gold. The female figure wore blue and white robes and held a gold caduceus in one hand and in the other a silver shield bearing in gold letters SPQR. At her feet is a wolf with the babies Romulus and Remus. The reverse was the same design, with the figure again facing the fly.

14th Regt of Infantry (See Fig 31) Eagle: silver. On the plaque, PULK 14/PIECHOTY (obverse) and WOYSKO/POLSKIE (reverse). Flag: 1st Battalion's was 77cm on stave by 56cm in fly. The obverse is blue with white eagle and gold lettering; the reverse crimson with gold lettering.

17th Regt of Infantry Flag: 52 by 56cm, crimson on both sides. On one side there is the white eagle, on the other a white circle enclosing the inscription PULK 17/IMIENIA/ZAMOYSKICH, and a white grenade in each corner pointing towards the centre.

1st Regt Voltigeurs de la Garde The only known details are a small square fanion listed by Andolenko, which bears in the top left and bottom right corners a flaming grenade; in the other corners a bugle horn. A crowned eagle of the Polish type, clutching very long lightning flashes, is in the top half of the centre, over a very large letter N, within two branches tied by a ribbon where they cross at the base. The embroidery is probably all silver, possibly in a red field.

1st Regt Chasseurs à Cheval Eagle: silver with silver crown, 28cm high by 50cm wide. This eagle has its wings widespread as if in flight and its head forward and turned towards its right wing. The plaque is dark blue with edging and lettering in silver; on the obverse POLSKIE, on the reverse WOYSKO. Standard: 60cm by 62cm with a 6cm silver fringe. Both sides are crimson with the same design: a silver eagle 32cm high with silver crown, sceptre and orb. Above the eagle, also in silver, the inscription LEGIA I; below the eagle, I PULK LEKKI IAZDV (Jadzy). Cords were silver.

15th Lancers Standard: 57 by 55cm with a silver fringe 3cm wide. Both sides were crimson with in the centre a silver eagle with crown, sceptre and orb also in silver. In the bottom corner of the fly was XV in silver. Cords were silver.

Amongst other Polish troops fighting alongside the French during the 1804–15 period were those of the Vistula Legion in the French Army. The flags carried by the 2nd Regiment of the Legion and the 1st Regiment of Lancers of the Legion are illustrated in Plates H3 and H4 respectively.

In November 1806 a small unit of about 100 horsemen was formed as a Garde d'honneur and in January 1807 was attached to the Imperial Guard as the 1st Regt of Polish Chevaulegers. By the decree of 6 April 1807 the regiment was incorporated into the Imperial Guard as the Régiment de Chevaulegers polonaise de la Garde (redesignated Chevaulegers lanciers in February 1810). The

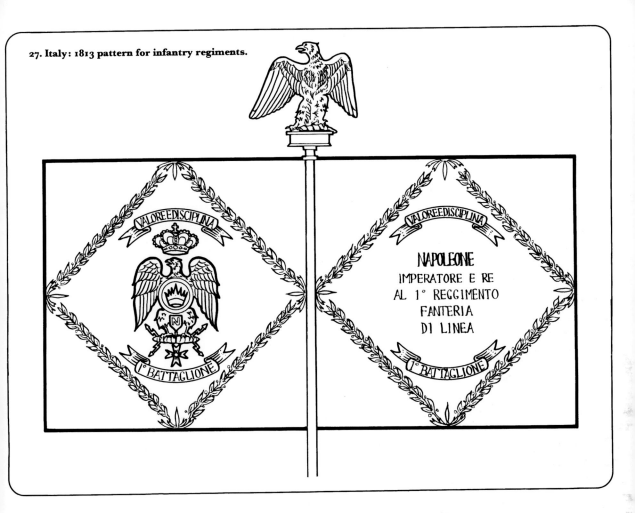

27. Italy: 1813 pattern for infantry regiments.

VALORE E DISCIPLINA

1° BATTAGLIONE

VALORE E DISCIPLINA

NAPOLEONE
IMPERATORE E RE
AL 1° REGGIMENTO
FANTERIA
DI LINEA

1° BATTAGLIONE

fanions carried by the squadrons of this regiment are illustrated in Fig 32. The squadron of 120 men which accompanied Napoleon to Elba in 1814 bore an 80cm square white standard with a gold fringe and a crimson bend (diagonally across the standard from the canton to the bottom fly) bearing three gold bees. The reverse may have had three golden Imperial crowns over the letters N instead of the bees. Cords were gold, cravat crimson and white, embroidered and fringed in gold. The finial was a gilt pike head, but may later have been changed to an eagle: see Fig 5 in the French section.

The Plates

A1 France: 1804 pattern
Obverse of the 1804 pattern, issued on the scale of one per battalion or squadron to all regiments of Line Infantry and Cavalry. The reverse was of the same pattern but bore on the central diamond L'EMPEREUR / DES FRANCAIS / AU er RÉGIMENT/D'INFANTERIE/DE LIGNE (or LÉGÈRE), the cavalry regiments bearing their respective titles in the bottom two lines, DE CUIRASSIERS, DE DRAGONS, DE HUSSARDS etc. For Guard regiments the dedication ended DE LA GARDE/IMPERIALE.

A2 France: 1812 pattern
Obverse of the 1812 pattern, issued on the scale of one per regiment to all Line Infantry and Cavalry regiments. The reverse was of the same pattern but bore in the place of the dedication the battle honours of the regiment. The 4th Légère was

entitled to bear ULM/FRIEDLAND at this date.

A3 France: 1815 pattern
Obverse of the 1815 pattern, issued on the scale of one per regiment to all Line Infantry and Cavalry regiments. The flags of the cavalry and dragoon regiments had fringes. The reverse bore the regiment's battle honours as on the 1812 pattern, with those extra honours gained in the later campaigns.

A4 France: Régiment Irlandais
Obverse of the flag presented to the Régiment Irlandais in 1804. The reverse followed the same pattern, but carried in the centre the inscription LIBERTE/DES/CONSCIENCES/INDEPENDANCE/DE L'IRLANDE surrounded by a yellow border charged with green wreaths. The regiment became the 3rd Foreign Regiment in 1811. The flags of the 2nd, 3rd and 5th Battalions remained green but bore only a single large golden harp in the centre: no details are known of the other battalions' flags or when this new pattern was issued. By the time of the 1813 campaign the regiment had received French flags of the 1812 pattern.

B1 and B2 France: Régiment d'Elite Gendarmerie à Pied
Obverse (B1) and reverse (B2) of the 1804 pattern carried by the dismounted half-battalion of Gendarmes d'Elite à Pied until their disbandment in 1806. The mounted branch carried from 1804 to 1811 a standard of similar design but with on the reverse an eagle with folded wings under an Imperial crown, with VALEUR ET DISCIPLINE beneath Jupiter's spindle. (The posture of this eagle varied from corps to corps within the Guard: see C1).

B3 France: Marins de la Garde
Reverse of the flag of the Marins de la Garde, issued in 1805 and carried until 1811. The obverse was of the same design but bore on the central diamond the dedication L'EMPEREUR/DES FRANCAIS/AU BATAILLON/DE MARINS/DE LA GARDE/IMPERIALE. The plinth below the eagle bore an anchor instead of a number.

B4 France: Horse Artillery of the Guard
Reverse of the guidon carried by the Artillerie à Cheval de la Garde from 1806 to 1813. The obverse was of the same design with in the central diamond the dedication L'EMPEREUR/DES FRANCAIS/AU RÉGT D'ARTILLERIE/À CHEVAL/DE LA GARDE/IMPERIALE. The plinth below the eagle bore the words Garde/Imperiale.

C1 France: Dragoons of the Guard
Reverse of the guidon carried by the Dragoons of the Guard from 1804 to 1811. The obverse was of the same design but bore in the central diamond the dedication L'EMPEREUR/DES FRANCAIS/AU RÉGIMENT/DES DRAGONS/DE LA GARDE/IMPERIALE. The standard carried by the Grenadiers à Cheval was of identical design, including the posture of the eagle, but in an 80cm square standard form. The dedication on the obverse of their standard read L'EMPEREUR/DES FRANCAIS/AU RÉGT DE GRENADIERS/À CHEVAL/DE LA GARDE/IMPERIALE.

C2 France: Mameluks of the Guard
Reverse of the guidon carried by the Mameluk troop (attached to the Chasseurs à Cheval de la Garde) from 1804 to 1811. The obverse was of the same design but bore in the central diamond the inscription L'EMPEREUR/DES FRANCAIS/A LA COMPAGNIE/DE MAMELUK/DE LA GARDE/IMPERIALE.

C3 France: 14th Dragoons
Obverse of the guidon carried by Line dragoon regiments from 1804 to 1812. The reverse was of the same design but bore in the centre the inscription VALEUR/ET/DISCIPLINE/ er ESCADRON.

C4 France: 11th Chasseurs à Cheval
Obverse of the standard carried by cavalry and dragoon regiments in 1815. The reverse bore the regiment's battle honours. In the case of the 11th Chasseurs à Cheval these were (up to 1812) Ulm, Austerlitz, Jéna, Eylau, Friedland, Eckmühl and Wagram.

D1 Baden: 3rd Regiment of Line Infantry
Basic pattern for obverse and reverse of all Baden infantry flags during the period 1806–15. The flags of the regiments were distinguished by various colours, the Leibfahne being in regimental facing colour with a white cross overall, the Regi-

menterfahnen in white with a cross of the facing colour.

D2 Baden: Light Dragoons
Obverse of the standard of the Baden-Durlach light dragoon contingent, transferred to Baden from Bavaria in about 1803 as a result of a border adjustment. The standard bears the arms of both states, and may originally have had a red field.

D3 Bavaria: 1808 Infantry pattern
Pattern for obverse and reverse of Leib- and Ordinärfahnen for infantry from July 1808. Leib-fahnen of this pattern were issued in 1809 to the Leib, 2nd and 11th Regiments; in 1811 to the 7th and 8th Regiments; and in the same year Leib- and Ordinärfahnen to the 4th Regiment.

D4 Bavaria: 1st Kürassier Regiment
Reverse of the 2nd division standard of the 1st Kürassier Regt, raised in 1814. (Cavalry regiments

were divided into three divisions.) The obverse was of the same design but bore in the centre the crest shown in D3.

E1 Berg: Infantry pattern 1809–13
Obverse of the pattern issued to infantry and cavalry regiments of the duchy in 1809, when Napoleon assumed the regency. The number in the top corner indicates regiment, that in the bottom corner the battalion.

E2 Hesse-Darmstadt: Leibfahne 1804–12
The three Hessian regiments all carried flags of this basic pattern, based on a flag captured at Wagram in 1809. (The one taken at Badajoz in 1812 had a XLL cypher). Each battalion had two flags, the 1st Battalion having the Leibfahne, which was white with black/red corners for the Leib-regiment, black/yellow for Erbprinz. The Leib-regiment's Regimenterfahnen were black with red corners, those of Erbprinz black with yellow corners. The

28. Italy: 1813 pattern for Guard infantry regiments.

Leib-Garde regiment carried all white flags. Size: 130cm square.

E3 Saxony: Infantry pattern 1810–13

Reverse of the basic pattern for Line Infantry, here bearing the border and in the colours of the Prinz Anton Regiment. Full details of field and border variations are given in the section on Saxony; the central emblem for the obverse is shown in E4.

E4 Saxony: Garde du Corps

Obverse of the Leibstandarte of the Garde du Corps, four of which were issued to the regiment in July 1811. Three were lost during the retreat from Moscow. The reverse bore the gold crown and cypher FAR within green branches.

F1 Westfalia: Infantry pattern 1808–13

Flags of the French pattern were issued at the rate of one per battalion in 1808; size 90cm square. The obverse was as illustrated except a JN cypher replaced the stars and the inscription was in French (LE ROI/DE WESTPHALIE/AU er RÉGIMENT/ D'INFANTERIE/DE LIGNE.) The reverse read VALEUR/ET/DISCIPLINE/ er BATAILLON. In 1810 German inscriptions were introduced: the reverse now read TAPFERKEIT/UND/GUTES BETRAGEN/ BATAILLON. New flags issued in 1813 had Gothic lettering, the regiment's number in the corner wreaths, and no laurel leaves round the central diamond.

F2 Westfalia: 1st Hussars 1812–13

The 1808 cavalry standards were of the same basic pattern as the infantry flags but 60cm square, with gold fringes and the cypher HJN in the corner wreaths. The reverse bore the coat of arms as illustrated. The inscription for the Gardes du Corps read DER KONIG/VON WESTPHALIEN/AN SEINE LEIBGARDE/ZU PFERDE. In 1812 the pattern was

30. Polish troops: Flag and eagle carried by the 2nd Battalion, 13th Infantry Regiment, from 1807.

PULK 13 PIECHOTY

SP QR

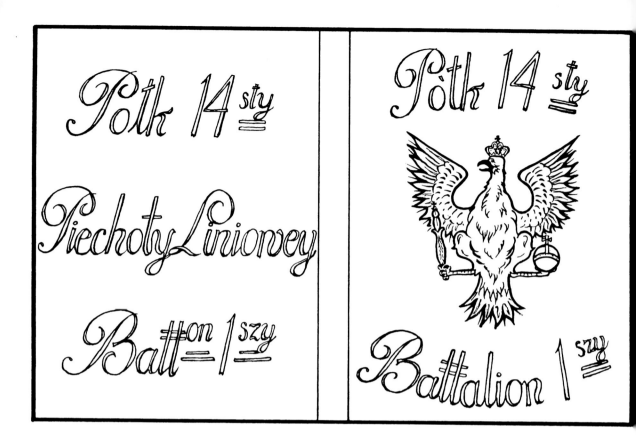

31. Polish troops: Flag carried by the 1st Battalion, 14th Infantry Regiment from 1807.

changed to a white saltire on a blue field as illustrated, with eagles in the blue triangles. The Gardes du Corps still bore the same inscription, with the arms as illustrated on the reverse and the cypher HN in place of the eagles.

F3 Naples: 1811 Infantry pattern
The reverse pattern carried by all infantry and cavalry regiments of the Neapolitan army of Murat from 1811 and possibly from as early as 1809. The obverse is illustrated in the section on Naples.

F4 Naples: 1806 Infantry pattern
Basic pattern for the obverse of all infantry flags from 1806 to 1809. The reverse, bearing the arms of the kingdom, is described in the section on Naples, along with regiment inscriptions.

G1 Italy: Grenadiers of the Royal Guard
Obverse of the flag issued to the Grenadiers of the

Royal Guard in 1805. The reverse carried in the centre the inscription GARDE ROIALE/VALEUR/ET DISCIPLINE.

G2 Italy: 1809 Infantry pattern
Obverse of the 1809 pattern issued to Line and Light Infantry regiments. The reverse is illustrated in the section on Italy.

G3 Italy: Gardes D'Onore
Reverse of the standard, 55cm square, issued to the Guards of Honour squadrons in 1813. The obverse was similar but bore instead of the central design the inscription GUARDIA REALI/D'ONORE. Above the inscription was a blue scroll with in gold VALORE E DISCIPLINA and below a similarly coloured scroll bearing 1º SQUADRONE (The 1st Squadron's is the only 1813 standard for the Guards of Honour to survive).

G4 Italy: 1st Cacciatori a Cavallo
Reverse of the standard, 60cm square, issued to Light Horse regiments in 1813. The obverse was similar but without corner emblems and in place of

32. Polish troops: 'Fanion' of the Régiment de Chevaulegers polonaise de la Garde: the obverse is shown above, the reverse below. Cream (probably white) field with light blue panels parallel to stave; all lettering and edging, silver. Obverse, white star and green laurel on red disc, light blue outer ring. Reverse, silver eagle on red star on light blue disc.

the eagle and scrolls bore the dedication NAPOLEONE/IMPERATORE E RE/AL 1º REGGIMENTO/CACCIATORI/A CAVALLO. Only the standards of the 1st and 2nd Regiments have survived.

H1 Duchy of Warsaw: 4th Line Infantry
Obverse of the flag carried by the 4th Infantry. The reverse was light blue and bore the same design but with an inscription along the edge of the fly: see in the Polish section of the main text.

H2 Duchy of Warsaw: 6th Line Infantry
Obverse of the flag carried by the 6th Regiment of Infantry. Reverse not known but possibly of the same design.

H3 Polish Troops: Légion de Vistule
Obverse of the flag carried by the Vistula Legion's 2nd Regiment. This flag had originally belonged to the 1st Polish-Italian Legion (from which the Vistula Legion was formed in 1807) and is of the pattern normally associated with the Revo-

lutionary Wars period. The 2nd Regiment was carrying this flag in early 1812, but it is not known if the flag was actually carried on the Russian campaign. The reverse was as the obverse except the lower scroll bore the battalion's number: eme BATAILLON.

H4 Polish Troops: Lanciers de Vistule
Reverse of the standard carried by the Lancers of the Vistula Legion in Spain, 1808–12. This is one of four standards issued to the Polish Legion in November 1800, which the Lancers of the Vistula Legion were authorised to carry in 1809. (The regiment became the 1st Regt of Lancers of the Vistula in 1810.) Two of these standards survive. There are two unusual points in these standards: firstly, the regiment never received an eagle, despite its fine record, but continued to carry these old standards until at least 1810: and secondly, these standards therefore in 1810 still bore the revolutionary symbols of a bonnet of liberty and lictor's fasces.

INDEX

Figures in **bold** refer to illustrations.